香港國際詩歌之夜 *2011*
INTERNATIONAL POETRY NIGHTS IN HONG KONG

編輯 Editors

方梓勳 Gilbert C. F. Fong
陳嘉恩 Shelby K. Y. Chan
柯夏智 Lucas Klein
何潔賢 Amy Ho Kit Yin
北島 Bei Dao

西川
Xi Chuan

目錄 Contents

1　某人 Somebody 2

2　鄰居 The Neighbors 6

3　我藏着我的尾巴 I Bury My Tail 12

4　無關緊要之歌 A Song of No Matter 16

5　牆角之歌 A Song of the Corner 18

6　熟人 Friends 20

7　伴侶 Companion 22

8　我奶奶 My Grandma 24

9　黃毛 Manes of Yellow 26

10　連陰雨 Drizzle 28

11　六朝鬼魅 Six Dynasties Ghosts 34

12　南詔國梵文磚：仿一位越南詩人
　　A Sanskrit Brick from Nanzhao (738–937):
　　after a Vietnamese poet 38

13　獵鷹、天鵝與珍珠 Falcons, Swans, and Pearls 40

某人

春天留在帽子裏
秋天留在布衫裏
早晨留在樹梢上
傍晚留在毛坑裏

荒山留在荒山上
碧水留在茶壺裏
豪宅留在地圖上
窮人留在陰溝裏

三斤墨汁留在腸子裏
一兩虛汗留在血管裏
唾沫留在店鋪外
髒話留在象牙上

紅留在紅臉上
白留在白臉上
香和甜留在嘴唇上
鹹和辣留在筷子上

怨留在左心室之西
憾留在泥丸宮之東
欲留在雞巴之前
困留在眼皮之後

病留在野郎中手心
痛留在野狐狸肩頭
奪命的雷電留在頭頂
一雙破鞋留在屋頂

肥皂留在天邊
狗屎留在花間
鬼魂留在板凳上
影子留在酒盅旁

空留在鏡子裏
風留在火苗上
《古文觀止》留在菜譜下
皇帝留在電視上

吞吞吐吐留在痰盂裏
三心二意留在棋盤上
俠肝義膽留在煙塵裏
一了百了留在枕頭上

Somebody

Spring stays inside the hat
Autumn stays inside the blouse
Morning stays on the treetops
Evening stays in the shithole

The barren mountain stays on the barren mountain
Jadeite water stays in the teapot
The mansion stays on the map
The poor stay in the gutter

Three pounds of ink stay in the intestines
50 grams of sweat stay in the bloodstream
Spit stays outside the store
Foul language stays on ivory

Red stays on a red face
White stays on a white face
Fragrant and sweet stay on lips
Salty and spicy stay on chopsticks

Scorn stays west of the left ventricle
Remorse stays east of the pubis
Desire stays in front of the dick
Exhaustion stays on the eyelids

Sickness stays in the palm of the quack
Heartache stays on the shoulder of the fox
Life-snatching lightning stays on top of the head
A pair of worn shoes stays on the roof

Soap stays at the edge of the sky
Dogshit stays in the flowers
Ghosts stay on the bench
Shadows stay beside the wineglass

Emptiness stays in the mirror
Wind stays on the flame
The Compendium of Classical Prose stays under the menu
The Emperor stays on TV

Stammering and sputtering stay in the spittoon
Being of two minds stays on the chessboard
Chivalry and gallantry stay in the dust
All's well that ends well stays on the pillow

(Translated by Lucas Klein)

鄰 居

我的鄰居。我從未請他們吃過飯，我從未向他們借過錢。我暗下決心，如果我有女兒，絕不讓她嫁給他們之中的任何人，因為他們幾乎像我的近親。

我能肯定他們住在我邊上（住得太近，就在隔壁），但我不能肯定他們是一些鳥、一些兔子，還是一些狐狸（就像我不能肯定我自己是個甚麼東西）。

我們交換過對於物價、天氣、中學生校服的看法，但我們從未交換過對於一個過路女孩的印象。我們交換過香煙和傳染病，我們將繼續交換香煙和傳染病。

隔壁女人每經過我的房門，便會朝屋裏張望。我關上房門，就能聽到她消遣打嗝一如消遣歌唱。

她和她丈夫，在他們的房間裏，肯定各佔對角線上一個牆角：兩人之間保持最大的距離，使家庭秘密保持疏朗的氣息。

但我承認，我不關心他們靈魂的問題，或他們有無靈魂的問題。

鄰居是偷聽者、竊笑者、道德監督者。我因監督鄰居的道德狀況偶然高尚，而他們以傳遞小道消息的方式向我傳遞時代精神。

時代精神鼓舞老張，把房子租給三個姑娘。三個姑娘畫濃妝，三個姑娘肚子疼，三個姑娘白天睡覺，傍晚洗臉，夜晚站在大街上。

時代精神鼓舞小李和小李，男人一和男人二，摟在床上，嬉笑，哭泣，做遊戲。

大麻和大蟠，像蜜蜂，蜇我的後背，嗡嗡嗡。我回頭看見她們笑，她們發我一包耗子藥。她們問我：「吃了嗎？」我説：「耗子吃了就行了！」

半夜，耗子們圍到我的床邊，齊聲招呼我：「你好，老鄰居！」我叫牠們全滾蛋。在這個家裏我説了算。

我家漏雨，必是所有的鄰居家都漏雨；我家斷電，必是所有的鄰居家都斷電。我走在38度的空氣裏，所有的鄰居也走在38度的空氣裏；我在自己的家裏脫衣服，彷彿是在所有的鄰居家裏脫衣服。

牆壁太薄，我聽見隔壁一家人再看電視連續劇《空鏡子》。我連夜加厚牆壁，壘起一堵新牆，第二天晚上還是聽見了《空鏡子》的主題曲。

我縮在屋裏連續七天不説話，不哼歌，不放屁，隔壁女人推門進來，為的是看看我的生活是否出了問題。

The Neighbors

My neighbors. I've never invited them over for dinner, never borrowed money from them. I promise myself that, if I have a daughter, I will never let her marry any of them, since they're like family.

I'm sure they live beside me (they live too close, right next door), but I'm not sure whether they're birds and rabbits, or if they're foxes (any more than I'm sure what I am).

We've exchanged views on prices, the weather, and school uniforms, but we've never exchanged our impressions of a girl crossing the street. We've exchanged cigarettes and communicable diseases, and we keep on exchanging cigarettes and communicable diseases.

Each time the woman next door passes by my door, she peeks inside. Closing the front door, I heard her hiccup to pass the time like she might sing to pass the time.

She and her husband, in their room, must stand at the wall diagonal from each other: with the greatest possible distance between them, their family secrets can maintain an air of openness.

But I admit, I don't care about their spiritual questions, or if they have any spiritual questions.

The neighbors are eavesdroppers, snickerers, moral monitors. Monitoring the morality of my neighbors I've happened upon nobility, but they let me in on rumors to let me in on the zeitgeist.

The zeitgeist emboldened Old Zhang, who rented the apartment to three girls. The three girls wear on heavy makeup, the three girls have stomach aches, the three girls sleep during the day, wash their faces in the evening, and stand on the street at night.

The zeitgeist emboldens Little Li and Little Li, Man One and Man Two, cuddling in bed, giggling, crying, playing games.

Momma and Auntie, like bees, sting my back, buzz buzz buzz. I turn around to see them smile, giving me a packet of rat poison. They ask: "Have you eaten?" I say: "What matters is if the rat's eaten!"

Rats, surrounding my bed at midnight, call me in unison: "Hello, old neighbor!" I tell them all to get lost. Under my roof you play by my rules.

My roof leaks, so all my neighbors' roofs must leak; power's out at home, so the power must be out in my neighbors' homes. I walk in 38° air, and all my neighbors walk in 38° air; I take off my clothes in my home, as if I were taking off my clothes in the homes of my neighbors.

The walls were so thin, I could hear the neighbors watching the miniseries Empty Mirror on TV. That night I thickened the walls, putting up another wall, and the next night I could still hear the theme song to Empty Mirror.

For seven days straight I holed up at home without speaking, or humming, or farting, and the woman from next door pushed the door open, just to see if something was wrong with my life.

(Translated by Lucas Klein)

我藏着我的尾巴

我藏着我的尾巴，混跡於其他藏着尾巴的人們中間。

我俯下身來，以為會接近我的影子，但我的影子也俯下身來，擺出一付要逃跑的姿勢。

喝一肚子涼水就能淹死全部的心裏話。

走着，我攤開手，但我不祈求世間任何東西。但是，啊，有甚麼東西會自動落入我的掌心？

碎玻璃割破手指，不見蚊子飛來。

我練習雙眼，練得像鷹眼一樣銳利。終於可以看清一切，內心的無奈便無法逃避。

如果你走得太近，我就用不上望遠鏡了。我的望遠鏡專為看你而準備，你應該僅僅呆在遠方。

街上的花瓣，是否西施的碎指甲？

我幹過的蠢事別人再幹，我無法阻止。我自己再幹一遍，只是想顯示我詭計多端。

既不能站在瘋子一邊對常人之惡束手無策，也不能站在常人一邊對瘋子之惡束手無策。

聰明人趕在天黑以前用完一天的理智。

抬頭望月,我猛按車鈴,同時忍不住像馬一樣朝月亮噴出響鼻。月亮上真安靜。

星期二,吹熄的蠟燭上一縷青煙。

星期三,南方的蒼蠅打敗了北方的蒼蠅。

我用汽車尾氣招待聚會的老鼠。牠們心滿意足,一致同意:世界真該死,而牠們不該死。

別嚇唬人,去嚇唬不是人的人吧,他們需要被嚇唬,就像他們需要被討好。

我用硬幣在你的皮膚上壓出圖案。

你計算天空的重量。玩一玩,行。你若認真,我就只好把你掐死。

夜晚的遊蕩者,我們避免相識。

I Bury My Tail

I bury my tail, taking my place amongst everyone else burying their tails.

I bend down, thinking I could approach my shadow, but my shadow bends down, too, getting ready to sprint away.

Drink a bellyful of ice water and you'll drown all the voices in your head.

Walking, I unfold my hands, but am not praying for anything on earth. But, oh, what will fall on its own into my outspread palms?

A shard of glass slices a finger, an unseen mosquito flies over.

I train my eyes, train them to be eagle-eye sharp. Finally seeing everything clearly, my heart's dead-end will have nowhere to run.

If you come too close, I can't use my telescope. I set it up just to watch you, so you should keep your distance.

Petal on the street, are you not Xi Shi's broken fingernail?

If others repeat my foolish mistakes, I can't stop them. If I repeat them, it's just to show how cunning I can be.

Neither able to stand by the mad with hands tied by the evil of the sane, nor able to stand by the sane with hands tied by the evils of the mad.

The intelligent hurry to use up a day's reason before nightfall.

Looking up at the moon, I fiercely ring my bicycle bell, and at the same time can't keep from snorting at the moon like a horse. On the moon it's very quiet.

Tuesday, a thin strand of smoke above the blown-out candle.

Wednesday, a fly from the south defeats a fly from the north.

With car exhaust I receive a gathering of mice. Their hearts and minds are satisfied, and in accord: the world is damned, but they are not.

Don't scare people, go scare those people who aren't even people, since they need to be scared, just like they need to be kissed up to.

I chart a map on your skin with a coin.

You calculate the weight of the sky. For fun, fine. But if you mean it, I'll have to pinch you to death.

Wanderers in the night, we avoid meeting each other.

(Translated by Lucas Klein)

無關緊要之歌

蒼蠅叫不叫「蒼蠅」無關緊要
它的嗡嗡聲越來越大無關緊要
它喝了一肚子墨水撒出的尿全是藍的無關緊要
它決定作一只優秀的蒼蠅無關緊要

我們兩人鴉雀無聲

蒼蠅飛走，房間裏多了一個人無關緊要
他談笑風生自得其樂無關緊要
他說他的聰明足以在天上吃得開，然後就走了
他是否成了天上最聰明的人無關緊要

我們兩人鴉雀無聲

鴉雀無聲的還不僅只我們兩人
還有窗外的電線杆和它移動的影子
電線杆上吊死一只風箏無關緊要
我們繞著電線杆跑了十萬八千里無關緊要

A Song of No Matter

Whether a fly is called "fly" matters not
That its buzzing is getting louder matters not
That it has a bellyful of ink and pisses blue matters not
That it has decided to be an exemplary fly matters not

You and I make not a peep

That the fly has flown away and someone else is in the
     room matters not
That he's chatting up a storm matters not
He says he's so smart they'll love him up in heaven, then
     leaves
Whether he'll be the smartest person in heaven matters
     not

You and I make not a peep

But not just you and I make not a peep
Nor do the telephone pole outside or its shifting shadow
That a kite has hanged itself on the telephone pole
     matters not
That we've run a hundred and eight thousand miles around
     the pole matters not

(Translated by Lucas Klein)

牆角之歌

我把一隻烏鴉逼到牆角
我要牠教給我飛行的訣竅
牠唱着「大爺饒命」同時卸下翅膀
然後掙脫我，撒開細爪子奔向世俗的大道

我把一個老頭逼到牆角
我要他承認我比他還老
他掏出錢包央求「大爺饒命！」
我稍一猶豫，他薅下我的金項鏈轉身就逃。

我把一個姑娘逼到牆角
我要她讚美這世界的美好
她哆嗦着解開扣子說「大爺饒命！」
然後把自己變成一只200瓦的燈泡將我照耀

我把一頭狗熊逼到牆角
我要牠一口把我吃掉
牠血口一張說「大爺饒命！」
我一掌打死牠，並且就着月光把牠吃掉

A Song of the Corner

I force a bird into the corner
I want it to teach me the trick behind flying
It sings out "Spare me, my master!" and removes its wings
Then it struggles to get free, splaying its claws toward the
    secular street

I force an old man into the corner
I want him to admit that I'm older than he is
Pulling out his wallet he pleads, "Spare me, my master!"
And in my hesitation he yanks off my gold chain and runs
    away.

I force a girl into the corner
I want her to praise the glory of the world
Shivering she undoes her buttons and says, "Spare me, my
    master!"
Then turns into a 200 watt bulb that shines its light on me

I force a bear into the corner
I want it to eat me up
It opens its bloody maw to say, "Spare me, my master!"
I smack it dead, and gobble it down in the moonlight

(Translated by Lucas Klein)

熟 人

張三請客，李四與王五同來。李四點菜。我們往死裏吃喝。推杯換盞之際我們談到近日的非典、禽流感、口蹄疫、瘋牛症。動物們瘋了，自殺式襲擊，但我們假裝頭腦清醒。我們感嘆即使感嘆理想主義已經過時的話題也已經過時。我們一起唱起舊日的歌曲，力爭唱出時代的新意。

王五付賬，我說謝謝。

他們三人眼睛裏漲出血絲。

我說謝謝。三人推開椅子將我圍攏。我覺出他們不懷好意，但不記得何時得罪過他們。

張三說：「咱們開始吧！」

我說：「幹嘛？」

李四打我一拳。

我說：「幹嘛？」

王五踢我一腳。

我說：「幹嘛？」

張三看着，將一口唾沫啐到我臉上。

我說「幹嘛？」

他們把我打得鼻青臉腫。他們終於有了吃飽的感覺。

我坐在地上堅持追問：「幹嘛？」

他們三人齊聲喝道：「你說幹嘛？」

Friends

Zhang is having company, Li and Wang come together. Li orders. We eat like our lives depended on it.

Between all the toasts and refills we talk about recent events, from SARS to the bird flu to foot-and-mouth to mad cow disease. The animals have gone crazy, attacking kamikaze-style, but we pretend we're still sober.

We sigh that it's passé to sigh over idealism being passé. We sing the songs of the old days together, vigorously singing the ideas of a new era.

Wang pays the bill, and I say thanks.

The three of them get bloodshot eyes.

I say thanks. The three of them push back their chairs and crowd around me. I sense they're up to no good, but can't remember when I offended them.

Zhang says: "Let's go!"

I say: "What are you doing?"

Li punches me.

I say: "What are you doing?"

Wang kicks me.

I say: "What are you doing?"

Zhang looks on, then spits in my face.

I say: "What are you doing?"

They beat me black and blue. Finally they've had their fill.

I sit on the ground and can't stop asking, "What are you doing?"

The three of them say in unison: "What do you think we're doing?"

(Translated by Lucas Klein)

伴 侶

我還不知道她是誰。

我還不知道她步入我的庭院推開我的房門是要找我還是要
　　找另一個人。

她爬上我的床，睡在我的不眠之夜，有如一截白蠟丟失了
　　她的火焰。

我抱起她來感覺翻越了一架高山。

半個月亮透過方形窗口照在我的前額，彷彿照在一個鬼影
　　朦朧的方形廣場，

至少那一夜我不曾侃侃而談，

我不想惹她討厭。

至少那一夜我幾乎不曾呼吸，

因為她深沉的呼吸表明她孤單又疲倦。

哦，不，沒有這樣一個「她」用深沉的呼吸表明她孤單又
　　疲倦。

沒有哪一夜我幾乎不曾呼吸否則我活不到今天。

我從不惹人討厭。

我從不侃侃而談那不是我的習慣。

我確曾漫步在方形廣場，但從未發現那裏鬼影朦朧。我只
　　允許圓滿的月亮透過圓形窗口將我的前額照亮。

我從未翻越過高山，即使在想像中。

我從不失眠，即使有白蠟把蠟油滴在我的眼瞼。

所以我不知道「她」是誰，這是當然。

Companion

I still don't know who she was.
I still don't know if she walked into my yard and opened
　　my front door searching for me or someone else.
She climbed onto my bed, sleeping through my insomnia,
　　like a white candle that had lost its flame.
Holding her and felt like crossing a mountain.
The half-moon shone onto my forehead through the
　　rectangular window, like shining on a public square
　　through a ghostlike haze,
at least that night I never spoke freely,
I didn't want to make her angry.
At least that night I barely breathed,
Because her heavy breathing proved she was lonely and
　　weary.
Oh, no, there is no "her" whose loneliness or weariness
　　could be proven with heavy breathing.
No night on which I barely breathed, or I wouldn't be alive
　　today.
I never make anyone angry.
I never speak freely it's not my style.
I have in fact strolled through public squares, but never
　　felt any kind of ghostlike haze. I only allow the full
　　moon to shine on my forehead through round windows.
I've never crossed mountains, never even imagined it.
And I'd never had insomnia, even if a white candle dripped
　　wax on my eyelids.
So I don't know who "she" is, that much is certain.

(Translated by Lucas Klein)

我奶奶

我奶奶咳嗽，喚醒一千只公雞。

一千只公雞啼鳴，喚醒一萬個人。

一萬個人走出村莊，村莊裏的公雞依然在啼鳴。

公雞的啼鳴停止了，我奶奶依然在咳嗽。

依然在咳嗽的我奶奶講起他的奶奶，聲音越來越小。

彷彿是我奶奶的奶奶聲音越來越小。

我奶奶講着講着就不講了，就閉上了眼睛。

彷彿是我奶奶的奶奶到這時才真正死去。

My Grandma

My grandma coughs, waking a thousand roosters.
A thousand roosters crow, waking ten thousand people.
Ten thousand people walk out of the village, the roosters
    in the village crowing still.
The rooster crowing stops, my grandma coughing still.
My still-coughing grandma mentions her grandma, her
    voice getting softer.
As if it were my grandma's grandma's voice getting softer.
My grandma talks and talks and then stops, shutting her
    eyes.
As if it were only now that my grandma's grandma really
    died.

(Translated by Lucas Klein)

黃 毛

「文明」和「進步」竟然首先呈現於小流氓的頭頂。這四個流裏流氣的男孩，這四個遊手好閒的男孩，這四個混混，這四個癟三，他們的黑髮染成黃毛，顏色由深而淺。他們在街上一字排開，朝前走，身後跟着三個女孩。陽光明媚。這三個女孩把時髦帶到這窮苦的鎮子上，把支攤賣桔子、香蕉的大嫂和大姐襯托得醜陋不堪。昨夜我看見他們，在小飯鋪裏喝酒。他們是小鎮上睡得最晚的人。他們是小鎮上最浪漫的人。韓國的風、日本的風，吹得他們變了質，他們成了不滿現狀的一伙、瞧不起別人的一伙、不能與環境打成一片的一伙。今天上午我又看到他們，從街這頭溜達到街那頭，然後又溜達回來。而這條街上，無非兩家飯館、一座小學校、一家旅館、一間郵局、一家藥店、一家魚店。魚店老板在不動聲色地宰殺一只白鵝。三個女孩中有一個女孩確有些姿色，但她的青春看來只能交給這黃毛中的一個。小流氓自有小流氓的福氣呵。小流氓自有小流氓的難處。

Manes of Yellow

"Progress" and "Civilization" appear even on the scalps of delinquents. These four boys of degeneracy, four boys of idle, roaming hands, four reprobates, black hair dyed into manes of yellow, color gone from dark to light. Four abreast on the street, marching forward, three girls in step behind them. Radiant sunlight. These three girls have brought vogue into this impoverished town, making the women selling bananas and clementines look hideous in comparison. I saw them last night, drinking in a noodle house. In the whole town they're the last to go to bed. In the whole town they are the most romantic. The winds from Korea and Japan have blown them into something else, making one a malcontent with how things are, making one disrespectful of others, making one unable to fit into society. This morning I saw them again, strolling from this end of the street to the other, and then strolling on back. But this street's no more than just a couple restaurants, a school, a motel, a post office, a pharmacy, and a fish shop. The owner of the fish shop butchers up a white goose without batting an eye. One of the three girls is kind of pretty, but she seems to have given her youth to one of those yellow-maned guys. Delinquency comes with its own delinquent delights. Delinquency comes with its own delinquent difficulties.

(Translated by Lucas Klein)

連陰雨

不是長頭髮——是長毛——是石頭上長毛 是麵包上長毛
是連陰雨
是連陰雨讓 衣服長毛 心靈長毛——這是衰朽的內驅力
讓木頭長出蘑菇 讓口腔長出潰瘍——同一種力量

讓愛長毛——愛 不是需要毛嗎？
讓抒情長毛——這才能顯現出不長毛的抒情——中老年的
　　抒情

長毛就是長醭——我媽說 就是發霉——我爸說
長毛在瓦片上 在夜晚11點以後的街道上
鐘錶的滴答聲——
雨說話的啞嗓子——
長出犯罪者 徘徊者 猶豫不決者——這是連陰雨的效果

淋濕的女人——

80天的連陰雨——還不算長久
80天的連陰雨覆蓋30萬平方公里的土地和大海——還不算
　　廣大

淋濕的女人孤獨而可憐——

是連陰雨 讓鞋子進水 濕了襪子——腳冰涼
然後水推進在人的身體裏
從下往上 頂到大腦——那裏一片汪洋

連陰雨下在汪洋大海之上——貨船駛向亞洲——雨下在日
　　本的庭院裏

有人老去　在中國——
雨下在遠離岸邊的工廠裏　下在鄉下
廚房的屋檐上　水滴滴個不停——飯菜備好　在不好不壞的
　　年頭

在不好不壞的年頭產生不好不壞的念頭——
有人死去
運氣不好的人　不甘心　遂移居到城裏——半個人不認識

窮人和富人　長一樣的毛
但富人並不擔心——可以扔掉長毛的東西——不包括他們
　　自己
好經濟和壞經濟　長一樣的毛
但好經濟知道　怎樣做長毛的生意——

能夠避開連陰雨的事物　避不開長毛
憤憤不平者的詛咒——

內在的生活膨脹——
海鷗和烏鴉　個頭巨大——
小超市裏的黃瓜　個頭巨大——這是連陰雨的緣故嗎？

門軸膨脹——開門的聲音——狗亂叫
狗亂叫的內驅力　也就是樓上腳步聲的內驅力
也就是衰朽的內驅力——朝向死亡的內驅力
表現在連陰雨之中　就是長毛

就是禿頂的人不長頭髮而長毛——這也就是新生
發霉然後新生——
在雨中——

這是連陰雨的力量，看吧——

（維多利亞 2009）

30

Drizzle

it's not fur—it's mold—mold on stones   mold on bread
it's drizzle
it's drizzle that makes   clothes grow moldy   the spirit
    grow moldy—this is the decay drive
making wood sprout mushrooms   making gums grow
    cankers—the very same force

making love grow mold—love   couldn't it use a bit of
    mold?
making the lyric grow mold—only this manifests the
    moldless lyric—the middle-aged lyric

mold's just mildew—my mom said   it's a fungus—my dad
    said
mold on the shingles   on the street after 11:00 P.M.
the tick-tock of the clock—
the hoarse voice the rain speaks in—
growing criminals   loiterers   waverers—these are the
    effects of drizzle

a wet woman—

eighty days of drizzle—not too long
eighty days of drizzle enveloping 120,000 square miles of
    land and sea—not too broad

a wet woman miserable and alone—

it's drizzle   that soaks shoes   that drenches socks—
    freezing feet
and then the water pushes into our bodies
from bottom to top   up into the brain—and all a vastness
    once there
drizzle falling on vast seas—cargo ships sailing to
    Asia—raining on Japanese courtyards

some grow old   in China—
raining on factories far from the coastline   raining on the
    plains
on the kitchen overhang   water's nonstop drip-drop—food
    prepared   in an age neither fair nor foul

an age neither fair nor foul producing notions neither fair
    nor foul—
some die
the unlucky   the unwilling   migrate to the cities—where
    they don't know a soul

rich and poor   both get moldy
but the rich don't worry—they can throw away whatever
    gets moldy—aside from themselves
a fair economy and a foul economy   both get moldy
but the fair economy knows   how to make money off mold

those things that can avoid the drizzle   can't avoid mold
curses of the indignant—

a swelling of interior life—
seagulls and crows   huge in size
cucumbers at the grocer's   huge in size—is it from all
    this drizzle?

hinges swelling—the sound of opening doors—dogs
    barking madly
the drive of dogs barking madly   which is the drive of
    footsteps upstairs
which is the decay drive—the thanatos drive
manifest in the drizzle   that is mold

the bald man with no hair but mold—this too is a new life
mildew and then a new life—
in the drizzle—

this is the force of drizzle, look—

(Victoria, 2009)

(Translated by Lucas Klein)

六朝鬼魅

六朝，公元265-588，鬼魅的數量超過了人口。活人夜晚夢見鬼魅，白天遇見鬼魅。鬼魅不避天光，猶如老鼠不避活人。六朝人的生活古古怪怪：據《幽冥錄》，連鬼魅也長着汗毛、腋毛和陰毛。鬼魅與人爭搶飯食。鬼魅之間打架鬥毆。

六朝鬼魅有學問，可以與人論《五經》，可以與無神論者辯論有無鬼魅。
六朝鬼魅神通大，知道每一個皇帝何時生，何時死，何時天下有大亂。
六朝男人在鬼魅的幫助下，遊了仙境游地府，回來之後掄小說。
六朝男人有艷福，但艷福也是鬼魅給的：女鬼們在墳中設宴，總有男人躬逢其盛。
六朝女人原形畢露時，就變回白鷺和白鵠，總之一個「白」字，透着血管隱隱。
六朝白鵠心腸好，追人追出五六里，遞上他丟失的鞋子。
但六朝老虎別出心裁，趁男人在屋外撒尿咬他的雞雞。

六朝人說，在我們那個時代，動物變人如家常便飯，可那個憂鬱的甚麼甚麼卡夫卡，少見多怪，讓人變成動物——肯定是寫撐了！肯定是寫錯了！

Six Dynasties Ghosts

In the Six Dynasties (265–588 CE), ghosts outnumbered humans. The living would dream of evil spirits at night and meet them in the day, the way that mice are never free from people. Life in the Six Dynasties was bizarre: according to The Chronicle of the Netherworld, ghosts had chest hair, underarm hair, and pubic hair. People and ghosts would fight over food. Ghosts and ghosts would come to blows.

In the Six Dynasties ghosts were educated, and could discuss The Five Classics with humans and debate atheists about the existence of ghosts.

In the Six Dynasties ghosts had powerful magic, and knew the birthdates of each emperor, plus their death dates, and when rebellion would break out under heaven.

In the Six Dynasties, with the help of ghosts, men would travel to faerie and the underworld, and write fiction when they came back.

In the Six Dynasties men had successful romances, but the successes were due to ghosts: female ghosts would host banquets in the grave, and what man wouldn't put in an appearance?

In the Six Dynasties when a female ghost's true nature was exposed, she would turn back into a white egret or swan, or anything white, through which veins would faintly show.

In the Six Dynasties swans were kindhearted, and would pursue a person for five or six miles, just to give back his slipper.

But in the Six Dynasties the tigers were the contrarians, waiting for men to take a piss outdoors so they could bite off their dicks.

Six Dynasties people say, Back in our day, animals turning into people was an everyday affair, but that lugubrious so-and-so Kafka, always making much ado about nothing, wrote about a guy turning into an animal—obviously he got it backwards! Obviously he got it mixed up!

(Translated by Lucas Klein)

南詔國梵文磚：仿一位越南詩人

大理古城玉洱路上一家古董店。古董店中一塊南詔國晚期的青磚。青磚上的十一行梵文。用模子壓出這十一行梵文的手。將這塊青磚砌進佛塔基座的手。認識這十一行梵文的南詔國晚期的高僧。將梵文從印度經尼泊爾傳播至南詔國的一個人或幾個人。佛教徒。大徹大悟的佛教徒或死前尚未大徹大悟的佛教徒，以及對大徹大悟了無興趣的浪蕩鬼。小乘佛教所遇到的大乘佛教不曾遇到的難題。南詔國皇帝所經歷過的不曾為大唐皇帝所知的痛苦。南詔國滅國的黃昏。擠倒佛塔的暴徒。驚愕的群眾。公元902年。從那時到現在，無數個我尋找過這塊壓有十一行梵文的青磚。在大理古城玉洱路上的這家古董店裏，我患着感冒，流着清鼻涕，從玻璃櫃裏取出這塊青磚，端在手上，最後跟店小二從800元殺價至430元。要是我一鬆手，它就會落到地上摔成數瓣。但我只曾有此念頭在一瞬間。當時在場的另有詩人宋琳和一只自屋樑垂絲下掛的蜘蛛。

A Sanskrit Brick from Nanzhao (738–937): after a Vietnamese poet

An antiques shop on Jadestream Rd. in Dali's old quarter. A grey-green brick in the shop from the late Nanzhao era. Eleven lines of Sanskrit on the grey-green brick. The hands that molded the Sanskrit lines. The hands that inlaid the brick into the base of the pagoda. The late Nanzhao monk who could read the eleven lines of Sanskrit. The man or men who brought Sanskrit from India through Nepal to Nanzhao. Buddhists. Buddhists who had or had not achieved nirvana before dying, and the loiterers who couldn't give a damn about achieving nirvana. The questions Hīnayāna Buddhism never encountered when encountering Mahāyāna Buddhism. The pain the emperor of Nanzhao suffered unbeknownst to the emperor of Tang. The dusk of Nanzhao kingdom's demise. The thugs who knocked over the pagoda. The astonished onlookers. 902 CE. From then till now, countless I's have searched for this grey-green brick molded with eleven Sanskrit lines. In this antiques shop on Jadestream Rd. in Dali's old quarter, coming down with a cold and with a runny nose, I pulled the grey-green brick out of the glass case, held it in my hands, and in the end talked the clerk down from 800 to 430 RMB. Just by shifting my hand, I could have dropped it and seen it shatter into shards. But I only had such a notion for an instant. Also present were the poet Song Lin and a spider dangling off a thread hanging from the rafters.

(Translated by Lucas Klein)

獵鷹、天鵝與珍珠

大遼國的皇帝熱愛珍珠，為此他的部下一次次攻打彼時尚未建國的北方大金國的土地。大金國並不盛產珍珠，但該土地上棲息和飛翔的獵鷹是大遼國的軍人們所垂涎的。一次次，大遼國的軍人們把獵鷹帶回家，順便帶回大金國的女人。他們把女人關進自己的房間，他們讓獵鷹去捉天鵝。大遼國的軍人們具備基本的生產知識：他們不在乎天鵝具有比他們屋裏的女人更優美的體態，但知道天鵝貪戀蚌肉的鮮美。幸好天鵝們只會傻吃蚌肉，卻把蚌內珍珠留在肚子裏──偶爾也會將珍珠連同大便一同排出體外。大遼國的軍人們向天空撒出獵鷹，等待獵鷹從渤海邊上捕回天鵝，然後取出天鵝肚子裏的珍珠。大遼國有的是天鵝，從未有人為殺幾只天鵝而多愁善感。他們殺天鵝的感覺跟殺雞的感覺差不多。他們留下中號珍珠帶給自己的女人，堆起小號珍珠用以和南方那些有錢的、玩物喪志的宋朝人做買賣。他們通常將大號珍珠獻給皇上，否則皇上會像他們殺天鵝一樣割下他們的頭顱。皇上玩着自己的珍珠，越玩越像玩物喪志的宋朝人。他就把大遼國玩到了滅亡。北邊的大金國興起了，不再送獵鷹了，同時也不再讓自己的女人被搶走。為了不再送獵鷹，大金國滅了大遼國。

Falcons, Swans, and Pearls

The Emperor of the Liao loved pearls, for which his troops time and again attacked the lands in the north that would later be established as Jin. Pearls were not in fact bounteous in the Jin, but the falcons that made nest and flew over that land were what the Liao soldiers coveted. Time and again, the soldiers of the Liao would bring home falcons, bringing home Jin women while they were at it. Locking the women in their rooms, they set the falcons after swans. Liao soldiers knew the basics of the forces of production: they didn't mind that swans had a more exquisite physique than the women in their rooms, since they knew the swans hungered after the delicacy of mussels. Good thing swans would go after mussels with such aplomb, they'd get the mussels' pearls down in their bellies— sometimes even expelling the pearls in their shit. The Liao soldiers would cast the falcons into the sky and wait for them to bring back swans from the Bohai Sea, when they'd pluck the pearls from their bellies. The Liao teemed with swans, and no one ever felt sentimental about having to kill one or two. Killing swans felt to them the same as killing chickens. The midsize pearls they kept for their women, while the small pearls piled up to trade with the rich hedonists of the Southern Song. They would have to bestow the biggest pearls unto the Emperor, or the Emperor would cut off their heads just as they did to the swans. The Emperor would play with his pearls, and the more he played the more he grew like the Southern Song hedonists. He played the Liao into extinction. When the Jin rose in the north, and sent no more falcons, they also stopped letting their women be kidnapped. The Jin destroyed Liao, to keep from sending more falcons.

(Translated by Lucas Klein)

詩人、隨筆作家、翻譯家，1963年生於江蘇，1985年畢業於北京大學英文系。現為北京中央美術學院中國古典文學教授。系美國艾奧瓦大學2002年訪問學者、紐約大學2007年附屬訪問教授、加拿大維多利亞大學2009年奧賴恩訪問藝術家、香港浸會大學2010年訪問作家。西川出版有四部詩集、兩部隨筆集、一部論著、一部詩文選、一部詩劇，另外還翻譯有龐德、博爾赫斯、米沃什等人的作品。其詩歌和文章被收入多種選集並被廣泛翻譯。曾獲1994年現代漢詩獎、1997年聯合國教科文組織阿奇伯格獎修金、2001年魯迅文學獎、2003年莊重文文學獎、1999年德國魏瑪全球論文競賽十佳獎等。

Born in 1963 in Jiangsu province, and graduated from the English Department of Peking University in 1985, Xi Chuan was Visiting Fellow at the University of Iowa, USA (2002), Visiting Adjunct Professor at New York University (2007), Orion Visiting Artist at University of Victoria, Canada (2009), and Visiting Writer at Hong Kong Baptist University (2010). He is now professor of classical Chinese literature at the Central Academy of Fine Arts in Beijing. Xi Chuan has published four collections of poems, two books of essays, one book of critique and one book of selected works, in addition to a play and numerous translations, including works of Ezra Pound, Jorge Luis Borges and Czeslaw Milosz. His poetry and essays have been widely anthologized and translated. He won various prizes, honors and fellowships like the Modern Chinese Poetry Award (1994), UNESCO-ASCHBERG bursaries of artists (1997), National Lu Xun

Prize for Literature (2001), Zhuang Zhongwen Prize for Literature (2003). He was awarded one of the top ten winners by the Weimar International Essay Prize Contest (Germany, 1999).

出版 Publisher
香港中文大學出版社 The Chinese University Press

封面及平面設計 Cover and Graphic Designer
朱德華 Almond Chu

製稿及分色 Art Work and Colour Separation
明星鐳射分色有限公司 Star Laser Graphic Co. Ltd.

印刷 Printer
宏亞印務有限公司 Asia One Printing Ltd.

出版日期 Date of Publication
二零一一年十月 October 2011

國際書號 ISBN
978-962-996-528-0

香港國際詩歌之夜2011主辦單位
International Poetry Nights in Hong Kong 2011 Organizers

香港中文大學東亞研究中心
Centre for East Asian Studies, The Chinese University of Hong Kong

香港城市大學人文社會科學院
College of Liberal Arts and Social Sciences, City University of Hong Kong

香港科技大學人文社會科學學院
School of Humanities and Social Science,
The Hong Kong University of Science and Technology

香港國際詩歌之夜2011協辦單位
International Poetry Nights in Hong Kong 2011 Co-organizer
木刻文化出版有限公司 MUKE Publishing Limited